About the Author

John F. Rappold jr. is a passionate storyteller with a knack for weaving whimsical tales that spark joy and imagination in young readers. Growing up in a suburb of Philadelphia, John has always had an active & creative imagination Inspired by growing up as a middle child with 2 older and 2 younger siblings. The Little Ghost and The New Friend is John's debut book crafted to delight children and families alike. When not writing, John enjoys spending time with his loving wife and family. John is also a devoted police officer where he serves and protects his community. The Little Ghost and The New Friend is inspired by John's childhood days spent growing up in a home with a creaky attic that seemed to whisper and creak all on its own, John imagined a friendly ghost hiding among the shadows, longing for a playmate. This sparked the heartwarming tale of an unlikely friendship between The Little Ghost and The New Friend.

Dedication

To my childhood attic, where creeks and shadows whispered tales of friendly ghosts, and to every young dreamer who believes in the magic of new friends.

— John

On the edge of the quiet, peaceful little town, where the trees whispered secrets and the wind sang forgotten songs, there stood an old house.

Inside the house, there was a tiny ghost named Wisp. He lived among echoes of laughter and stories from long ago, making the place warm and full of memories.

Wisp was not like the other ghosts. He was not a scary ghost. He did not rattle chains or moan during the night like most of the other ghosts.

He was different. He loved to float through the halls, peacefully watching the moonlight dance on the dusty floors. But in the beauty of everything, he found himself completely alone, feeling quite lonely.

One autumn evening, as another day passed and Wisp was sitting all alone.

He noticed something different. There was a flicker of light coming from the abandoned house next door, sparking curiosity and a hint of mystery. Someone had moved in! His curiosity sparked like a cozy, warm candle flame, inviting a sense of wonder and comfort.

Peeking through the cracked window, he noticed a young girl happily unpacking boxes. She had bright eyes and a soft scarf wrapped warmly around her neck, giving her a cheerful and inviting appearance. Maybe, Wisp quietly whispered to himself, I could have a friend too.

That night, Wisp made an effort to introduce himself, in hopes of finally making a new connection. He floated gently into her room, making sure not to startle her.

But just as he was about to say hello, she suddenly turned! She gasped in surprise as Wisp disappeared suddenly into thin air.

The girl furrowed her brow as she looked around with a curious and slightly concerned expression.

"Hello?" she asked. Wisp hesitated for a moment and then whispered back, "Hello?"

Instead of screaming, the girl smiled warmly. She asked curiously, "Are you a ghost?"

"Yes," Wisp said softly, a gentle blush on their cheeks. "Are you feeling a little scared?"

She shook her head with a friendly, confident smile. "No, not at all. My name is Penelope. Pepper for short."

Penelope happily told Wisp all about her old home, her love for books, and how sometimes she felt lonely, too. Wisp listened, with a warm heart, feeling as bright as a lantern shining in the night.

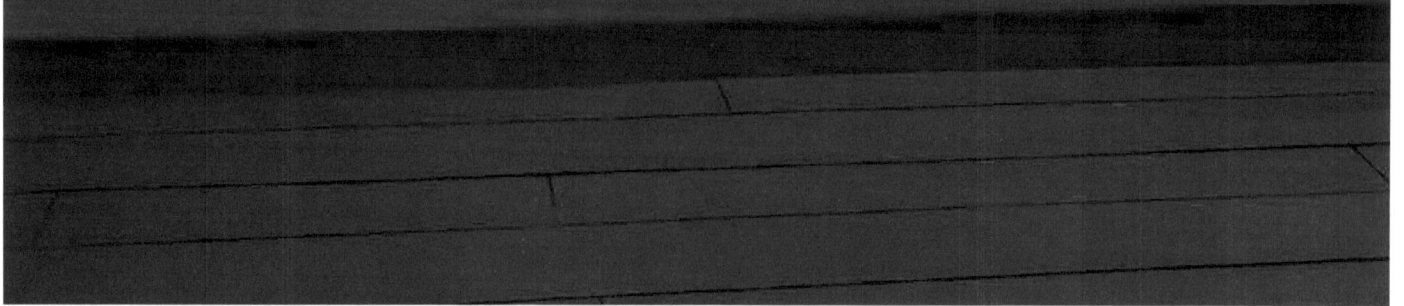

Over time, they grew closer and spent almost every moment together. Wisp eagerly showed Penelope the hidden secrets and wonders of the house, the secret staircase, the paintings that whispered, and the attic filled with shimmering stardust. It was a magical tour that filled her with wonder and joy.

Penelope happily showed Wisp how to play shadow puppets by candlelight, sharing a lovely moment. He, in turn, brought the shadows to life in ways that no human ever could, creating a mesmerizing dance that captivated everyone.

On a very chilly night, Penelope softly whispered, "I was afraid to move here. But now, with you, I feel at home."

Wisp beamed brightly, feeling more like a friend than just a ghost for the very first time.

As autumn transitioned to winter, their friendship blossomed into something warm and unshakable, strengthening with each passing day. Wisp finally felt seen. He no longer felt invisible. It was a comforting feeling to have someone who saw him, truly saw him.

In the old house on the edge of town, under the gentle glow of the moon, a little ghost and a lonely girl found something neither had before, a forever friend. It is a sweet reminder that sometimes, the most unexpected friendships can light up our lives.

www.ingramcontent.com/pod-product-compliance
Lightning Source LLC
LaVergne TN
LVHW072132070426
835513LV00002B/73